Celebrate the Sponge!

10th Birthday Editon

SCHOLASTIC INC.
New York Toronto London Auckland
Sydney Mexico City New Delhi Hong Kong

Stephen Hillenburg (signature)

Based on the TV series *SpongeBob SquarePants*® created by
Stephen Hillenburg as seen on Nickelodeon®

No part of this publication may be reproduced, stored in a retrieval system,
or transmitted in any form or by any means, electronic, mechanical, photocopying,
recording, or otherwise, without written permission of the publisher.
For information regarding permission, write to Simon Spotlight,
an imprint of Simon & Schuster Children's Publishing Division,
1230 Avenue of the Americas, New York, NY 10020.

ISBN-13: 978-0-545-20280-0
ISBN-10: 0-545-20280-9

The SpongeBob SquarePants Trivia Book
ISBN-13: 978-0-439-24247-9 • ISBN-10: 0-439-24247-9
Copyright © 2000 by Viacom International Inc.

Dear SpongeBob . . . A Funny Fill-ins Book
ISBN-13: 978-0-439-53974-6 • ISBN-10: 0-439-53974-9
Copyright © 2003 by Viacom International Inc.

Jokes from the Krusty Krab
ISBN-13: 978-0-439-76817-7 • ISBN-10: 0-439-76817-9
Copyright © 2005 by Viacom International Inc.

Bikini Bottom Riddles
ISBN-13: 978-0-439-72425-8 • ISBN-10: 0-439-72425-2
Copyright © 2005 by Viacom International Inc.

All rights reserved. Published by Scholastic Inc., 557 Broadway, New York,
NY 10012, by arrangement with Simon Spotlight, an imprint of
Simon & Schuster Children's Publishing Division. NICKELODEON,
SpongeBob SquarePants, and all related titles, logos, and characters are registered
trademarks of Viacom International Inc. Created by Stephen Hillenburg.
SCHOLASTIC and associated logos are trademarks
and/or registered trademarks of Scholastic Inc.

12 11 10 9 8 7 6 5 4 3   9 10 11 12 13 14/0

Printed in the U.S.A.   40

First Scholastic printing, September 2009

Table of Contents

TRIVIA BOOK

BY
DAVID FAIN

Avast there, mateys! Here's the rarest sea creature of them all—SpongeBob SquarePants! He may look like an ordinary sponge to you landlubbers, but take my word for it, he's the most unique talking yellow cube filled with holes you'll ever find on the ocean floor—or any floor for that matter.

I'm READY

Hi! I'm SpongeBob SquarePants! And I'm ready to start another wonderful day here in Bikini Bottom. I'm ready, I'm ready, I'm ready! Whoops! Look at the time! I still have to do my morning workout, eat a healthy breakfast of Kelpo, and feed my pet snail, Gary, before I go to work.

FRIENDS and NEIGHBORS

I've got lots of neat friends. Let me introduce you to some of them.

Patrick is my best friend. We do everything together: jellyfishing, blowing bubbles, playing superheroes, hunting for pirate treasure, you name it. He also likes sleeping, drooling, and lying dormant under his rock.

Sandy is a land squirrel, which means she has to wear a hat full of air and a pressure suit to live underwater. She's a great surfer and an excellent karate expert, just like me! She's from this faraway place called Texas. That's why she talks the way she does. Don't worry, you get used to it after a while.

That's my next door neighbor, Squidward Tentacles. Even though we work all day together at the Krusty Krab, I never get tired of spending time with him. He practices his clarinet a lot, although he never seems to get any better. He doesn't have time to play with Patrick and me. We practically have to drag him out of his house kicking and screaming just to get him to have some fun.

Mr. Krabs is my boss, and the owner of the Krusty Krab restaurant where Squidward and I work. People say he's cheap, but I consider it an honor to work for the creator of the Krabby Patty! Sometimes I think that maybe I should be paying him!

AROUND
BIKINI BOTTOM

Patrick's rock

two-story pineapple

Easter Island head

Here's where we live. The two-story pineapple is mine. It's fully equipped with a shellphone, state of the art stuffed animal barbells, and a foghorn alarm clock. Next door is my pal Squidward's Easter Island head, and next to that is my friend Patrick's rock. Every weekend I use my reef blower to keep my yard seashell free and sparkling.

Howdy, y'all! This is my house, the treedome! It's full of the driest, purest, airyest air in the whole sea! I have all the comforts of home: an exercise wheel, a picnic table, an oak tree, and a trampoline. The treedome is made of polyurethane (that's a fancy name for plastic).

9

BORN to COOK

Here it is, my work place, the finest eating establishment ever established for eating—the Krusty Krab! Home of that tasty, juicy, scrumptious, warm mouthful of steamy goodness called the Krabby Patty! Would you like fries with that?

Across the street is the Chum Bucket, owned by Mr. Krabs's archrival, Plankton! With the help of his computer, Karen, Plankton's always trying to steal the Krabby Patty recipe. People say he's evil, but I think he just needs a friend.

It's not that easy to become a member of the Krusty crew. You really need the expertise to properly prepare the perfect Krabby Patty.

First comes the bun, then the patty, followed by ketchup, mustard, pickles, onions, lettuce, cheese, tomatoes and bun—
in that order.

THE RENAISSANCE CEPHALOPOD

Hello, friends, and welcome to my private art gallery. I have conquered all artistic mediums in my pursuit of the perfect self-portrait. Being the only squid of culture in this backward community is a heavy burden, but one I could gladly bear if it weren't for the constant pestering of . . . SPONGEBOB SQUAREPANTS! I can't get a moment's peace from that nuisance and his equally annoying friend Patrick!

Do you know they come over every day (and twice on Sundays) to ask me if I want to go jellyfishing? Jellyfishing? Me? Have you ever heard of anything so ridiculous?!

And that's just the beginning! SpongeBob throws me birthday parties when it's not my birthday,

he's always making a racket,

and as if that isn't bad enough, he keeps leaving his undergarments on my front lawn!

BUBBLE-BLOWING TECHNIQUE

Wanna blow some bubbles? It only costs twenty-five cents. Here's your bubble wand, dipped and ready to go. Remember, it's all in the technique!

* **First, go like this.**
* **Spin around—stop!**
* **Double-take three times . . . one, two, and three.**
* **Pelvic Thrust—Woo Hoo!**
* **Stomp on your right foot. (Don't forget it!)**
* **Now it's time to bring it around town. Bring it around town!**
* **Then you do this, then this, and this and that and thisandthatandthisandthat!**

You can blow bubbles in all sorts of interesting shapes.
Try some of these:

A CUBE

DUCKS

A CENTIPEDE

A BUTTERFLY

A DANCE PARTNER

A TUGBOAT

AN ELEPHANT

You can also whisper messages inside the bubbles to send to your friends. Just be sure the right person gets the right message. Or that the message is from the right person. Or that the message goes to the person on your right. Or that you don't forget . . . oh, tartar sauce! I forgot who I was sending this message to!

CHAMPIONS
of the DEEP

You're just in time for my favorite television show: *The Adventures of MermaidMan!* I've got a genuine imitation copy of his uniform. Patrick says his young ward, Barnacle Boy, is better, but that's just because that's who he is when we play superheroes.

They are so cool! Patrick and I found out that MermaidMan and Barnacle Boy live over at the Shady Shoals older citizens' home. We think they're working undercover!

Recently roused from retirement, the aquatic avengers have launched a new series of adventures, though now much older (and considerably less wiser). Watch in awe as they:

CHANGE A LIGHTBULB!

WAIT FOR THE AQUAPHONE REPAIRMAN!

EAT THEIR MEATLOAF!

ADJUST THEIR HEARING AIDS!

PLAY CHECKERS!

TRY TO REMEMBER WHERE THEY PARKED THE INVISIBLE BOATMOBILE!

BOATING SCHOOL QUIZ

When I'm not working, I go to Mrs. Puff's Boating School. I can hardly wait until I get my license. If only I didn't always get so nervous during the driving exam. Oh well, you know what they say—thirty-eighth time's the charm! (Okay, thirty-ninth!)

Mrs. Puff is the best boating teacher I've ever had. Well, actually she's the only boating teacher I've ever had. She's a puffer fish (which means she has her own built in airbag, which comes in very handy during those driving tests). Let's see how much you know about boating.

1 The front of the boat is called the
a) bow.
b) porthole.
c) stern.

2 The first thing you do when you're about to start the driving test is
a) floor it!
b) put it in drive.
c) start the boat.

3 Red means
a) floor it!
b) stop.
c) make a right turn.

4 If you see a big anchor in the middle of the road, you should
a) floor it!
b) crash into it.
c) jump over it.

5 The second thing you do when you're taking the driving test is
a) pop a wheelie.
b) put it in drive.
c) cross the finish line.

6 If you see someone in the crosswalk while you're driving, you should
a) get out and help him or her cross the street.
b) turn around and go the other way.
c) go upside down.

7 In boating terms, right is
a) starboard.
b) port.
c) wrong.

8 If your boat has a kitchen onboard it's called
a) the keel.
b) the hall monitor.
c) the galley.

9 If you have a walkie-talkie inside your head and someone else is telling you what to do during the driving test, you are
a) lucky.
b) dreaming.
c) cheating.

10 The last thing you should do when you're taking the driving test is
a) watch Mrs. Puff being taken away in an ambulance.
b) cross the finish line.
c) floor it!

SQUIDWARD SEZ

Our pal Squidward is always claiming that he doesn't want to play with SpongeBob and me. We know he's just playing a game where he says the opposite of what he really means (just like on Opposite Day). Let me show you. First he'll talk, and then I'll translate.

WHEN SQUIDWARD SAYS:

"How did I ever get surrounded by such loser neighbors?"

HE REALLY MEANS:

"I have the best neighbors in the world!"

WHEN SQUIDWARD SAYS:

"You're killing me, SpongeBob ... you really are!"

HE REALLY MEANS:

"Do it again!"

WHEN SQUIDWARD SAYS:

"Can we lower the
volume, please?"

HE REALLY MEANS:

"Do it again . . . louder!"

WHEN SQUIDWARD SAYS:

"Oh, puh-leez!"

HE REALLY MEANS:

"You're welcome."

WHO SAID IT?

Hear me, surface dwellers! That simpleton starfish isn't the only one around here who knows something about language! I have created a foolproof device that allows me to perfectly imitate the voice of any resident of Bikini Bottom I choose! Don't ask how this will help me to obtain a Krabby Patty—it's far too complicated to explain to your miniscule mentalities. What I need from you is help in sorting out who says what! Match each sentence to the person most likely to have said it, and I may spare you when I destroy this miserable town!

1. "Mother O' Pearl!"   Ⓐ SpongeBob

2. "Sea creatures assemble!"   Ⓑ Patrick

3. "Is it already time to ruin Squid's day?"   Ⓒ Sandy

4. "Meow."   Ⓓ Squidward

5. "Ain't that just the bee's knees?"   Ⓔ Mr. Krabs

6. "You guys want to lift some weights?"   Ⓕ MermaidMan

7. "I'm ready!"   Ⓖ Gary

8. "Oh, my aching tentacles!"   Ⓗ Larry the Lobster

9. "Daddy, you're embarrassing me!"   Ⓘ Mrs. Puff

10. "Whose turn is it to be hall monitor?"   Ⓙ Pearl

ANSWERS:
1E, 2F, 3B, 4G, 5C, 6H, 7A, 8D, 9J, 10I

MUSSEL BEACH PARTY

This is Mussel Beach, where my friends and I sometimes go to have fun. Everyone has their own favorite things to do here, and at the nearby, wonderful, stinky mud puddle we call Goo Lagoon. I'll let them tell you themselves!

Well, I get really stoked from catching a wave! That's surfing, for all you nonaquatic wannabes. My favorite move is to do a handstand while shooting the tube. That way I can hang ten . . . fingers that is! I also enjoy playing Frisbee with my friends, although SpongeBob tends to try catching it with his face!

What I like doing at Goo Lagoon is lying on the sand and sleeping. Actually I like lying on the sand and sleeping anywhere. I don't even have to be on sand ... or even lying down. I just ... like ... zzz zzz zzz.

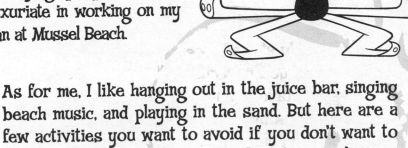

Well, if I wasn't always being bothered by certain very annoying people, I would luxuriate in working on my tan at Mussel Beach.

As for me, I like hanging out in the juice bar, singing beach music, and playing in the sand. But here are a few activities you want to avoid if you don't want to end up the biggest loser on the beach:

- Getting sand in your buns
- Forgetting your sunscreen (and getting sunburned)
- Being buried in the sand and getting left behind
- Ripping your pants (repeatedly)
- Pretending to drown

MAY I TAKE YOUR ORDER

THE KRUSTY KRAB, HOME OF THE ONE AND ONLY KRABBY PATTY!

Remember, at the Krusty Krab,

YOU ARE THE CAPTAIN!

SANDWICHES

$2.00

KRABBY PATTY

$2.50

DOUBLE KRABBY PATTY
WITH THE WORKS

KRUSTY COMBO KRABBY PATTY, FRIES, AND MEDIUM DRINK

$3.99

$3.00

KRUSTY DELUXE
DOUBLE KRABBY PATTY
WITH THE WORKS AND OYSTER SKINS

CRYING JOHNNIE
$2.25
KRABBY PATTY
WITH EXTRA ONIONS

$1.99

BUBBLE BASS SPECIAL
KRABBY PATTY HOLD THE PICKLES
(UNDER YOUR TONGUE)

$1.75

MINNOW MEAL
SEANUT BUTTER AND JELLYFISH JELLY
SANDWICH, FRIES, AND SMALL DRINK

SIDES

OYSTER SKINS . . . . $.50
FRIES $1.25
SEAWEED SALAD $1.50
CORAL BITS $1.95

DRINKS

SALTY SHAKES **$.99**

DR. KELP OR
DIET DR. KELP **$.89**

And don't forget, every Tuesday is Mouthful of Clams Day! Everyone who shows up with a mouthful of clams gets a free drink!

 # MONEY BACK GUARANTEE

THE SECRETS to SUCCESSFUL JELLYFISHING

Welcome to Jellyfish Fields, where wild jellyfish roam, just waiting to be captured. This is the best place in Bikini Bottom to go jellyfishing. Here are a few pointers for you beginners:

☺ Bring a good solid net. Be sure to name it. Mine's called "Ol' Reliable."

☺ Remember, SAFETY FIRST! Always wear your safety glasses.

☺ Firmly grasp the net.

☺ Always set the jellyfish free after you've caught it (you wouldn't like being kept in a jar either).

☺ It helps if you sing "La, la, la" or "Da, da, da, da dum" while you jellyfish.

☺ Disguise yourself as a piece of coral in order to get close to your prey.

☺ Watch out for those stingers!

The jellyfish who live in Bikini Bottom are completely different from all other jellyfish in the sea. For example, they make a loud buzzing sound when they swim, they live in hives, and produce a delicious strawberry-flavored jelly. There's nothing like the taste of natural jelly from a jellyfish.

Remember, these jellyfish aren't pets, they're wild animals. They have powerful electrical stingers and use them when angry. They love to dance, and can't resist a good solid beat. But be warned: they don't like clarinet music (at least they don't like the way Squidward plays clarinet music)!

SPONGEBOB'S BUSY SCHEDULE

Sometimes I have so much to do it's hard to keep it straight. I'm glad I've got someplace to write it all down!

Monday 11
Boating Exam today—don't forget to bring apple for Mrs. Puff. (Some bandages might not be a bad idea either.)

Sunday 10
Opposite Day. Be sure to act like Squidward.

Friday 15
15th of the month . . . Annoy Squidward Day! Call Patrick.

Saturday 16
Squidward's Birthday!

Sunday 17
Annual Jellyfish Convention in Ukulele Bottom. Find snail-sitter for Gary.

Tuesday 19

Have Squidward cover as fry cook. Make sure Krusty Krab is well-stocked with antacid tablets before leaving. Buy Mr. Krabs a gift to make up for loss in profits.

Wednesday 20

Squidward's Birthday!

Thursday 21

Glove World Grand Opening! Remind Patrick we need to stand in line all weekend to be sure we are the very first ones inside, just like last year.

Saturday 23

Sign Up Deadline for Mussel Beach Anchor Throw. Make sure to keep Sandy occupied and far away from Goo Lagoon. Prepare Karate ambush?

Sunday 24

Squidward's Birthday!

Tuesday 26

Employee of the Month Judging Begins. Break Squidward's alarm clock.

Wednesday 27

Anniversary of first Day met Sandy. Definitely prepare Karate ambush! Pay day. Buy Mr. Krabs a sympathy card.

Friday 29

Squidward's Birthday!

SNAIL CARE

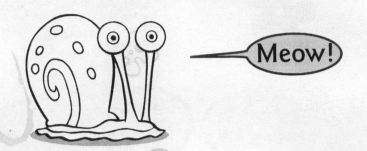

Meow!

Okay, I'll tell them, Gary. Gary wants me to let you know the most important information in the care and feeding of pet snails:

1. Snails need lots of food. They get one can of snail food in the morning and one can at night.

2. Don't let them get salty. Make sure they have plenty of water.

3. They need to be walked twice a day.

4. Snails love to play "fetch." Bring something to read, this can take awhile.

5. Your pet snail's "meowing" at the moon can annoy the neighbors. Try to keep it to a minimum.

6. Snails are natural-born poets. Encourage their artistic expression.

7. VERY, VERY IMPORTANT: Whatever you do, don't let yourself get accidentally injected with snail plasma.

DANGERS of the DEPTHS

Howdy, y'all. As Bikini Bottom's resident science expert, I'm here to tell y'all about a few sea critters you should give a wide berth to should they ever cross yer path:

Giant Clam. I tussled with one of these rascals myself the first time SpongeBob and I met. They're just big bullies. A few well-placed karate chops will more'n likely send them on their way with their tails betwixt their legs (if'n they had any legs, that is).

Nematodes (or undersea worms). These hungry little dudes don't look like much, but put a passel of them together and they can gnaw a coral reef down to a stub in ten seconds flat.

The Mother of All Jellyfish. This is the large economy-sized version of those cute little fellers who float out in Jellyfish Fields. But this mamma packs quite a wallop when it comes to stingers. Just ask Squidward.

Anchovies. Just like nematodes these little dudes ain't anything to be afraid of in small numbers, but fill a few tour buses with schools of these hungry fish, and they're as likely to stampede as look at ya! And to top it off, they're smellier than all get out.

Poison Sea Urchins. They're tiny and spiny and make you itch all over.

The Flying Dutchman. Although technically not a critter, he's more of a bogeyman ghost-type varmint. Anyhoo, he's as ornery as Mr. Krabs on payday and twice as ugly, so keep yer distance or he'll steal yer soul!

DID YOU KNOW?

Did you know that in Bikini Bottom—

Moss always points to civilization.

Through the misuse of time travel, Squidward invented the art of jellyfishing.

The specialty of the house at Plankton's restaurant, The Chum Bucket, is Chumbalaya. (No wonder he doesn't have any customers!)

SpongeBob has won the employee of the month award twenty-six months in a row.

The Flying Dutchman haunts the Seven Seas because he was never put to rest (people used his body for a window display after he died).

✳ In the future, everything will be chrome and there will be 486 letters in the alphabet (one for each SpongeTron clone produced).

☺ **Patrick knows a lot about head injuries.**

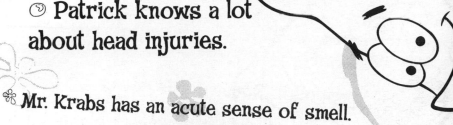

✳ Mr. Krabs has an acute sense of smell.

☺ **SpongeBob has had the following items inside his head:**

-A towel   -Plankton

-A walkie-talkie   -A lightbulb
(He makes a pretty good disco ball.)

✳ Squidward has a lifetime subscription to *Frown Digest Magazine.*

☺ **Souls look like pickles.**

✳ SpongeBob also plays a mean conch.

Did y'all know that up in the surface world . . .

✳ SpongeBob SquarePants series creator Stephen Hillenburg has a degree in marine biology as well as experimental animation.

෧ SpongeBob was originally named SpongeBoy, but someone was already using that name, so the "y" became a "b."

✳ Ernest Borgnine and Tim Conway provide the voices for MermaidMan and Barnacle Boy. This is the first time the two have worked together since *McHale's Navy*.

◎ Staff writer Mr. Lawrence contributes spoken as well as written words for the series. He performs the voice of Mr. Krabs's archrival Plankton, the announcer at sporting events in Goo Lagoon, and several others. (He's also the voice of Philbert the turtle on *Rocko's Modern Life*).

✳ Painty the Pirate (seen at the beginning of each SpongeBob SquarePants episode singing the theme song) has the live-action lips of series creator Stephen Hillenburg.

SING ALONG with PAINTY

Ahoy there, kids! Ready to sing the SpongeBob SquarePants theme song?

I can't hear you!

OOOOOOOOOOOOOOOOOOH, Who lives in a pineapple under the sea?
SpongeBob SquarePants!
Absorbent and yellow and porous is he.
SpongeBob SquarePants!
If nautical nonsense be something you wish,
SpongeBob SquarePants!
Then drop on the deck and flop like a fish!
SpongeBob SquarePants!
SpongeBob SquarePants!
SpongeBob SquarePants!
SpongeBob SquarePants!
Sponge— Bob, Square— Pants!
Ah ha ha ha ah har har har

Dear SpongeBob. . .
A Funny Fill-ins Book

by Steven Banks

Hi! It's me, SpongeBob SquarePants! I get a lot of letters asking important questions and I need your help answering them. Are you ready? Here's what you do . . .

Pick a friend to write words in the blanks. He or she will not read the letters out loud until all the blanks have been filled in. The other friend (or friends) will give him or her the words.

When asked for a NOUN, fill in the name of a person, place, or thing. *Clam, seaweed,* and *bucket* are examples of nouns.

When asked for a VERB, fill in an action word. *Eat, wrestle,* and *honk* are examples of verbs. You'll also be asked for an "-ing verb." This means words like *eating, wrestling,* and *honking.* Sometimes you'll be asked for a "past-tense verb." *Ate, wrestled,* and *honked* are examples of past-tense verb.

An ADJECTIVE is a word that describes a person or a thing, like *pretty, amazing,* or *horrible.*

An ADVERB is a word that describes how something is done, and usually ends with "ly," like *quickly, shyly,* and *seriously.*

You'll also be asked for specific words like "type of food," "type of sea creature," or "number." Just fill in a word that's one of those things.

That's it! I'm ready—let's go!

Dear SpongeBob,

I have a huge problem. I can't sleep at night. Every time I go to bed I hear a noise that sounds like a(n) ___bear___ trying to swallow a(n) ___fish___.

type of animal

noun

Help!

Signed,

Sleepless in Bikini Bottom

Dear Sleepless in Bikini Bottom,

That's just my friend Squidward playing his clarinet! I suggest putting ___meat stake___ in your ears or wearing a(n) ___hat___ over
type of lunch meat   *noun*

your head. If this doesn't work, drink a(n)___water___flavored glass of warm ___milk___.
    noun   *type of liquid*

You can also try counting ___all the seacresers___s
         type of sea creature

jumping over___a sail___s. That always works
      noun

for me!

Sweet dreams!

Sleepily yours,
**SpongeBob
SquarePants**

49

Dear SpongeBob,

I get very nervous when I have to take a test at school. The minute I sit down at my _____desk_____, my mind goes
noun

_____doner_____, and I forget
adjective

everything I _think imbad at. math_
past-tense verb

At this rate, I'll be in summer school for the next ___50___
extremely high number

years!

What can I do?

Signed,

Summer-School Bound

Dear Summer-School Bound,

I know how you feel! Whenever I take a test at Mrs. Puff's Boating School my _arm_ (body part) gets sweaty and my _arms_ (body part) shakes. Sometimes I can't remember the answers, so I just guess or put down the number _5_ (number). The last time I took my driving test I ran over a(n) _kid_ (noun), crashed into a(n) _bike_ (noun), and then drove back to school so slowly that an old _ganga sgh_ (type of sea creature) passed me. But someday I will pass the test and become a(n) _expert_ (adjective) driver!

Studiously yours,

SpongeBob SquarePants

RULES of the ROAD

Dear SpongeBob,

I want to be a great jellyfish hunter like you! I have a state-of-the-art net, but so far I've only caught ___1___
number

___Jelly___ ___fish___ s. What am
adjective   noun

I doing wrong?

Signed,

Jellyfish-Hunter Wanna-Be

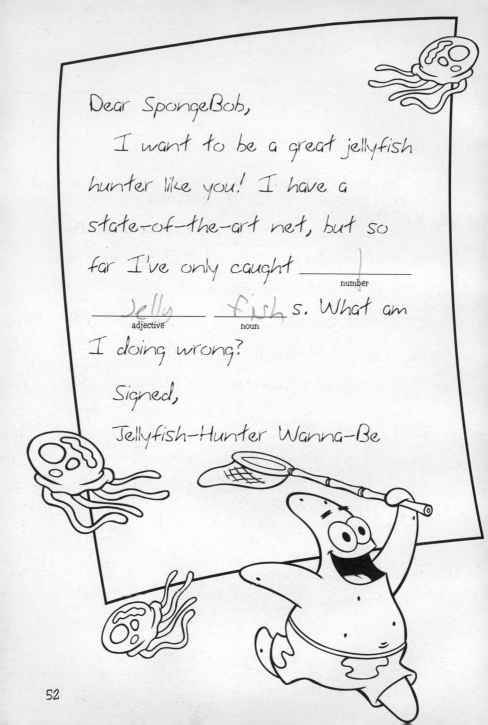

Dear Jellyfish-Hunter Wanna-Be,

You've come to the right place for advice—jellyfishing is my favorite sport! As the great jellyfish hunter _____ _____ once said: "The
a pet's name   a friend's last name
secret to becoming a(n) _____ jellyfish hunter is
adjective
having the _____ of a(n) _____ ,
body part   type of animal
the heart of a(n)_____ , the eyes of a(n)
type of insect
_____ , and the strength of a(n)_____ ."
type of bird   type of circus performer
I have no idea what that means but it seems to work

for _____ ! It also helps to have a good
same pet's name
battle cry that sounds like a(n)_____ . Just don't get
sound
stung. Once I got stung on my _____ _____
body part   number
times and I couldn't sit down for _____ weeks!
number

Your pal,

SpongeBob
SquarePants

P.S. Don't forget to let the

jellyfish go so you can catch

them again the next day!

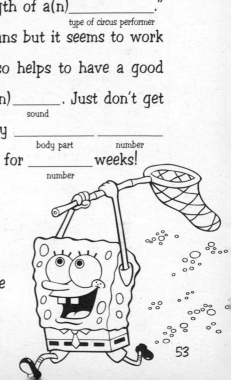

53

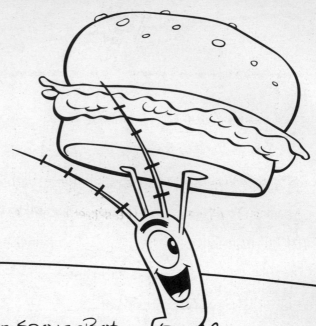

Dear SpongeBob,

I would like to know how to make the _____ Krabby Patties.
adjective
I promise not to tell anyone the secret recipe!

You can trust me,

Joe McSworkelsteen

Dear Mr. McSworkelsteen (if that's your real name),

I can never reveal the Krabby Patty recipe! Mr. Krabs made me take the sacred Krabby Patty oath of secrecy: "I swear I will never tell the secret of the Krabby Patties! If I do, may my _____ be tickled and my
<u>body part</u>
_____ be sprayed with hot_____, and
<u>body part</u>   <u>type of liquid</u>
may I soak in a bathtub full of _____ juice
                                 <u>type of vegetable</u>
and may wild_____s nibble at my toes, and
            <u>type of animal</u>
may _____ sing_____ in_____
     <u>a teacher's name</u>   <u>a song title</u>   <u>foreign language</u>
over and over till I turn _____and then make me watch
                          <u>color</u>
_____movies backward!" So you can understand
<u>movie star</u>
why I would never tell!

Your krabby pal,

SpongeBob
SquarePants

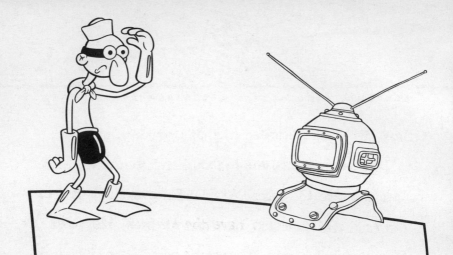

Dear SpongeBob,

I am a(n) _____ fan of
adjective

Mermaid Man and Barnacle Boy.

I hear you have a(n) _____
adjective

collection of their things. Can

you tell me about it?

Signed,

Mermaid Man Fan

Dear Mermaid Man Fan,

I have a rare Mermaid Man _____ that
                                    article of clothing
smells like a(n) _____ when you put it in
                        type of sea creature
_____. I also have the Mermaid Man watch
    type of liquid
that doesn't tell time because he never learned how. I

have the Barnacle Boy _____ with _____ spring
                            noun   adjective
action that makes it _____ _____ feet per second
                            verb   number
(batteries not included). I also have an autographed

Mermaid Man _____ and a Barnacle Boy
                    bathroom item
_____ that comes in _____ colors and goes
    noun   number
_____ when you throw it. My favorite thing is a piece
  sound
of Mermaid Man _____-flavored _____ that is
                    flavor   food item
_____ years old and still in perfect condition!
  number

Your super friend,

*SpongeBob
SquarePants*

Dear SpongeBob,

    I have a friend named SpongeBob
SquarePants! Isn't that _____
                                                     adverb
amazing? You both have the same name!
Signed,
Patrick Star

Dear Patrick,

It's me-your best_____ SpongeBob! When I
　　　　　　　　　noun
am not_____ overtime at the Krusty Krab,
　　　　·ing verb
I write an advice column for the *Bikini* _____
　　　　　　　　　　　　　　　　　noun
Times. We just talked about it yesterday, remember?

I told you about the big _____ in my office,
　　　　　　　　　　　　noun
the_____ phone with all the flashing lights,
　　adjective
and the supply closet that is filled with_____s.
　　　　　　　　　　　　　　　　　　　noun
Call me-we'll do lunch!

Best,
SpongeBob

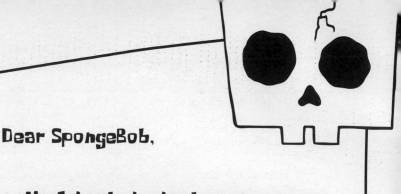

Dear SpongeBob,

My friends invited me to a scary movie but I'm too scared to go. I keep making up excuses like, "Sorry, I have to _____ my _____ —maybe
next time." But I'm running out of reasons. What should I do?

verb   noun

Signed,
Scaredy Cat

Dear Scaredy Cat,

Buy a _____-gallon box of popcorn and hide
             high number
behind it when the movie gets_____scary. The
                                    adverb
scariest movie I ever saw was *Attack of the*

_____-Foot _____-Shark Monster. It was about
 number   type of fruit
a shark named _____, who was very nice until
                a boy's name
a vampire _____ bit him. After that he turned
            type of insect
into a giant_____ every time the moon rose.
              noun
His girlfriend,_____, loved him even though he
                a girl's name
ate her _____, her favorite_____,
         musical instrument   noun
and all the_____s in the city. My friend Patrick
             noun
hid under his seat the whole time. He missed the

movie, but he found a lot of old _____ on
                                  type of food
the floor to snack on.

Your frightened friend,

**SpongeBob
ScaredyPants**

Dear Mr. SquarePants,

   I would like to get a job at the Krusty
Krab. I have a lot of experience in fast
food. I make excellent _____
                              type of fruit
and _____ sandwiches, delicious
         type of vegetable
fried _____ -balls, and the best
              type of food
_____ with seaweed sprinkles this
   type of dessert
side of the Pacific. Can you help me?

Sincerely yours,

Mr. P.

62

Dear Mr. P.,

I am afraid there are no job openings at the Krusty Krab. No one ever quits because it's the most _____ job in the world! When I'm _____ Krabby
_{adjective}   _{-ing verb}

Patties I feel like the king of the_____! And I don't
         _{a place}

just get to make the greatest burgers this side of _____, I get to sweep_____s under the rug,
_{a planet}   _{noun}

make the bathrooms extra_____, and watch Mr.
         _{adjective}

Krabs_____ his money!
_{verb}

Your krusty buddy,

SpongeBob SquarePants

63

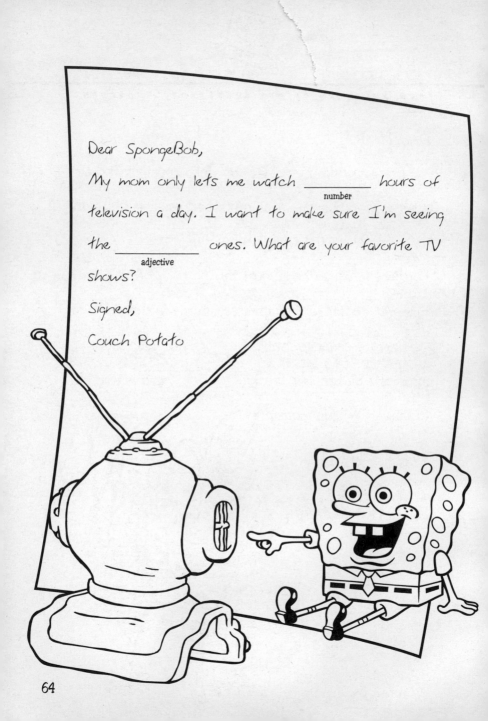

Dear SpongeBob,

My mom only lets me watch _____ hours of
                                    number

television a day. I want to make sure I'm seeing

the _____ ones. What are your favorite TV
      adjective

shows?

Signed,

Couch Potato

64

Dear Couch Potato,

My very favorite TV show is *Mermaid Man and Barnacle Boy*, but I also like *The_____ Man and*
<small>noun</small>

the_____ , _____ for Sand Dollars,
<small>type of fish</small>   <small>-ing verb</small>

The _____ Adventures of Jed _____
<small>adjective</small>   <small>type of fish</small>

_____ , How to _____ Your Snail,
<small>type of occupation</small>   <small>verb</small>

and *Everybody Loves _____ .*
<small>type of fish</small>

Your TV-loving pal,

SpongeBob SquarePants

Dear SpongeBob,

There's a bully at school who keeps bothering me. He_____s me when I walk by, _____ s my lunch money, and sometimes even stuffs me into a(n)_____! What should I do?

Signed,

Hiding in My Locker

Dear Hiding in My Locker,

Bullies are just nice people trapped inside mean

people's _____s. You could try to win him over by

       _{noun}

making him a(n) _____ or by inviting him to

           _{type of dessert}

_____ . Or you could do what I do when I see

  _{a place}

a bully: _____ away as fast as a(n)_____,

      _{verb}   _{type of animal}

screaming like a(n)_____ !

            _{type of bird}

Safe at home,

SpongeBob SquarePants

Dear SpongeBob,

Have you ever been to a rodeo? I am very curious about what goes on there. I hear it has something to do with _____ s _____
type of animal   -ing verb

_____ s around a ring. Is that true?
noun

Signed,

Rhinestone Cowboy

Dear Rhinestone Cowboy,

I have never been to a rodeo, but my friend Sandy

told me all about them. You wear _____
article of clothing

and chaps and _____ boots with pointy
type of occupation

toes and _____s on the heels. Then you ride a(n)
noun

_____ piggyback yelling 'yee haw' until he
type of animal

_____s you by_____you up and down. The
verb   -ing verb

object is to stay on the _____ for
same type of animal

_____seconds before getting _____across the
number   -ed verb

ring. Sounds _____ to me!
adjective

Yipee Yi Yay,

SpongeBob
SquarePants

Dear SpongeBob,

What kind of music do you like? I'm tired of all my_____s and would like some new_____s to listen to. Are there any_____s from Bikini Bottom that I should check out?

Signed,

Singing Fool

Dear Singing Fool,

I love music! One of my favorite bands is The

_____ _____ Experience. My
type of sea creature   type of fruit

favorite songs by them are "_____ in the
                              a girl's name

_____ with _____ s," and "If You Were My _____ I'd
noun   noun   noun

_____ with You All Day Long Except _____."
verb   day of the week

My friend Patrick's favorite band is The _____ -Note
                                          low number

Band. They only play _____ note(s) and they only
                     same number

know one song called "This Song Is Hard to Play." My

friend Sandy loves The Texas _____ Boots (featuring
                             adjective

Betty Sue _____ on _____). Squidward
          type of sandwich   musical instrument

likes The _____ -Clarinet Orchestra and Louis
          high number

_____ and the _____ Hot Clams.
type of fish   number

Musically yours,

SpongeBob
SquarePants

Dear SpongeBob,

I am throwing a party next week and I want it to be great. We're going to play pin the_____on the_____ , musical
<u>noun</u>   <u>type of animal</u>
_____s, and capture the _____ . But
<u>noun</u>   <u>noun</u>
I need help figuring out what else to do.

Any advice?

Signed,

Party Hearty

Dear Party Hearty,

The secret to a good party is good food, good music, and good friends! My favorite party foods are pizza with_____ and _____ on top,
<u>type of breakfast food</u>   <u>type of candy</u>

_____ cupcakes, and of course, Krabby
<u>type of lunch meat</u>

Patties. I know all the latest dance moves, so if you invite me to your fun party I'll show everyone how to do "The Funky_____," "The_____ _____,"
<u>noun</u>   <u>adjective</u>   <u>noun</u>

and "The _____ Twist." Most importantly, you
<u>type of hat</u>

need good friends at a party! They can help you clean up. And like my friend Patrick always says, "A party without friends is a like a _____ without a(n)
<u>noun</u>

_____ in the_____."
<u>car part</u>   <u>season</u>

Good luck,

SpongeBob
SquarePants

Dear SpongeBob,

I'm thinking about getting a pet snail.

Snails are so _____ and _____.
           adjective   adjective

Can you tell me about your pet snail,

Gary?

Signed,

I Like Gary

Dear I Like Gary,

Gary is _____ special! He's a purebred snail
　　　　　　adverb

directly descended from _____, the _____
　　　　　　　　　　　a boy's name　　　　　adjective

snail from the fourteenth century who saved the

_____ Wall of_____from burning down
adjective　　　　　　name of city

by sliming it. Gary can do_____ tricks! He can
　　　　　　　　　　　high number

jump over a(n)_____, he knows how to say "meow"
　　　　　　noun

in _____ languages, and he does a perfect imitation
　number

of _____ . Gary and I really like to play
　　movie star

hide-and-_____. I always hide in my_____
　　　　verb　　　　　　　　　　type of room

and he always finds me by using his _____ .
　　　　　　　　　　　　　　　body part

Gary is the greatest pet a sponge could have!

Your partner in slime,

**SpongeBob
SquarePants**

75

Dear SpongeBob,

Guess what? I am in the Mermaid Man and Barnacle Boy Fan Club too! We should meet up at the _____
a place
for a(n) _____ and _____
type of food   type of drink
and swap trading cards. What is your favorite Mermaid Man and Barnacle Boy adventure?

Signed,

MM & BB Forever

76

FROM THE DESK OF MR. SPONGEBOB SQUAREPANTS

Dear MM & BB Forever,

I love *all* the Mermaid Man and Barnacle Boy Adventures, but my favorite is "Mermaid Man Meets the ____________ (type of occupation) s of the ________ (adjective) Empire of Space Dinosaurs." It's the one where Mermaid Man is captured by Man Ray, put in a(n) ________ (type of pastry), and sent into space in a(n) ________ (noun). Meanwhile Barnacle Boy can't find Mermaid Man so he hangs up his ____________ (article of clothing) and gets a job at a(n) ________ (place of work) ________ (-ing verb) ________ (noun) s. Mermaid Man is turned into a(n) ________ (noun) and held prisoner inside a ________ (type of room) and forced to make ________ (type of toy) s. He escapes using a(n) ________ (kitchen item), and a space dinosaur named ________ (a girl's name) helps him build a space ship out of ________ (type of fruit) to return home! Mermaid Man finds Barnacle Boy, who is now selling ________ (noun) s door-to-door. The two heroes are reunited; they capture Man Ray and find out that he is Mermaid Man's ________ (type of relative) 's ________ (type of relative) 's ________ (type of relative) 's ________ (type of relative) 's best friend!

Up, up, and away!

SpongeBob SquarePants

Dear SpongeBob,

I keep having the same _____
adjective

nightmare about _____
a teacher's name

shrinking down to the size of a(n)

_____ and moving into my
type of insect

_____ drawer. Do you
article of clothing

ever have weird dreams?

Signed,

Dream Weaver

78

Dear Dream Weaver,

I had a(n) _____ _____ dream last night! I
                  adverb   adjective

lived in an oversized _____ and rode to work on
                              type of hat

a(n) _____. But I wasn't working at the
         type of animal

Krusty Krab—I had a job at the Chum Bucket! I had to

make plankton patties and sing songs about _____s!
                                                            noun

The plankton patties were made out of _____ flakes,
                                                      noun

_____ goo, and _____ chunks. I ate one and it tasted
  noun   noun

like a(n) _____. And then my friends walked in and
               noun

they all looked _____ weird! Patrick was a(n) _____,
                        adverb   noun

Sandy was a(n) _____, Squidward was a(n)
                      type of occupation

_____, and Gary was a man-eating _____.
  type of plant   type of bird

Boy was I glad to wake up!

Sleeping with one eye open,

**SpongeBob
SquarePants**

Dear SpongeBob,

Why are *you* of all people giving advice! / should be doing it! The readers need someone who is _____ smart and _____ intellectual!
<small>adverb</small>   <small>adverb</small>

I know about _____ in _____ , where
<small>-ing verb</small>   <small>a country</small>

_____ go to _____, and the difference
<small>type of fish</small>   <small>verb</small>

between _____s and_____
<small>type of vegetables</small>   <small>type of dance</small>

. . . unlike some people / know.

Signed,

Squidward

Dear Squidward,

I would love your help writing these letters! It would be the greatest thing since _____
<small>a famous person</small>

went _____ in_____ and discovered the
<small>-ing verb</small>   <small>a place</small>

first_____. There's plenty of room at my _____
<small>noun</small>   <small>type of furniture</small>

for both of us. We could sit side by side and go out for

_____ and eat with our _____s and take
<small>type of food</small>   <small>body part</small>

long walks in the_____together. We'll be joined at
<small>noun</small>

the_____–it'll be great!
<small>body part</small>

Your *pen* pal,

SpongeBob

Dear SpongeBob,

　　I want to get a surprise gift for my best friend. Last year I got him a(n) _____ –flavored _____
　　　　　　　　type of fruit　　　　　　　　　　article of clothing
and a pet _____. What do you
　　　　　　　　noun
think he would like? He is yellow and square and spongy.

Thank you,

Patrick Star

P.S. Don't tell
SpongeBob
I'm getting
him a gift!
It's a secret!

Dear Patrick,

Thanks pal, but you don't have to get me a gift!

Although I did like the _____ made out
type of board game

of _____ you gave me on _____ !
type of candy   day of the week

Your friend,

SpongeBob

Dear SpongeBob,

Is the Flying Dutchman real or imaginary? I made a bet with my friend that he's real. If I win the bet, she has to _____ my _____s until _____ verb noun _____; if she wins, I have to _____ month her _____s until _____! Can you verb noun month settle our bet?

Signed,

Fingers Crossed

Dear Fingers Crossed,

The Flying Dutchman is as real as a(n)_____!
<u>noun</u>

And so are Santa Claus, the Easter_____,
<u>type of animal</u>

the Tooth _____ , and the_____
<u>type of occupation</u>   <u>adjective</u>

_____ that goes_____ in the_____
<u>type of fish</u>   <u>sound</u>   <u>time of day</u>

and brings_____ to good little boys and girls!
<u>type of candy</u>

Your best bet,

SpongeBob
SquarePants

85

Dear SpongeBob,

You have a(n) ___freaky___ sense of
                   adjective

style—I just love the ___stinky___
                            adjective

fashions you wear. How can I become

a(n) ___smelly___ dresser like you?
           adjective

Signed,

Clothes Horse

Dear Clothes Horse,

Everyone should have a white shirt, tie, short pants, athletic socks, and shoes in their wardrobe! But when you play __hockey__ you should wear a(n)
_{type of sport}

__Mister__, tight __Black__ pants, and size_____
_{type of hat}   _{color}   _{size}

sneakers. If you go out on the town to_____
_{verb}

someplace fancy, you should wear a(n)_____
_{type of flower}

in your lapel and carry a(n)_____. And make
_{noun}

sure your shoes are_____and your socks are
_{adjective}

_____.
_{adjective}

All dressed up and

nowhere to _____,
_{verb}

*SpongeBob
SquarePants*

Howdy, SpongeBob!

How the _____s are you? I'm in Texas right now—the
           noun

_____ place in the world! You would love it here,
adjective

SpongeBob. They're having a(n) _____ Karate
                                    adjective

Jamboree, a(n) _____ rodeo, and a(n)
                  type of insect

_____ festival all in the same week! I'll bring
   type of dance

you a(n) _____-gallon cowboy hat, a giant box
           high number

of hot chili _____s, and some chocolate-covered
               food item

_____s shaped like a Texas _____. Wish
  noun   type of reptile

you were here!

Yee Haw,

Sandy

P.S. Don't forget to water my _____s and feed my
                                noun

_____s.
  noun

Dear Sandy,

That sounds _AWESOME_! I can't wait to hear all
adjective

about your _big_ trip! Take lots of _____s
adjective   noun

and hurry back, y'all!

Your karate-chopping buddy,

SpongeBob

89

Dear SpongeBob,

I got the lead _____ in my school
                       noun
play "The Importance of Being

_____." I am very nervous!
     type of sandwich

Help!

Signed,

Sweaty Palms

Dear Sweaty Palms,

Just relax and don't do what I did! I was in a play at the

Bikini Bottom _____ Theater called "King Neptune
                  type of meal

and the _____ _____ ." I had to wear a(n)
            adjective   noun

_____ made out of_____fur. My
   article of clothing   type of animal

sword got tangled in the fur and I tripped and fell on my

_____ . I started sweating like a(n)_____ .
 body part   type of sea creature

I only had one line: "I have a message for the king in my

pocket that must be sent to France by pigeon." Instead I

said, "I have a(n)_____ for the_____ in my
                  noun   type of occupation

_____ that must to be sent to _____ by
  article of clothing   a planet

a(n)_____." Patrick thought it was the_____
  type of fish   -est adjective

line he'd ever heard.

Your fellow nervous actor,

**SpongeBob
SquarePants**

Thanks for all of your help

with these letters-so long!

Ever your pen pal,

SpongeBob
SquarePants

NICK

SpongeBob squarepants

Jokes From the Krusty Krab

by David Lewman

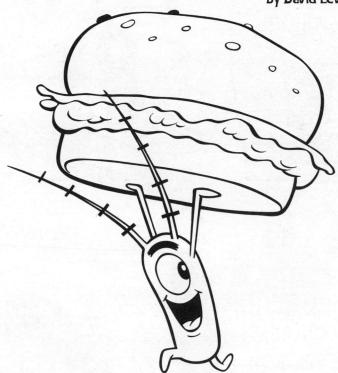

SpongeBob: What does food start out as?

Sandy: Baby food.

SpongeBob: What kind of food do you feed to sharks with your bare hands?

Squidward: Finger food.

When is food like Plankton?

When it goes bad.

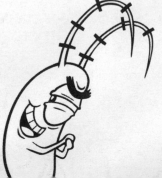

SpongeBob: Why do fishermen like to fish where there are tons of mosquitoes?

Sandy: 'Cause they get lots of bites!

SpongeBob: Why should you never eat in a dirty house?

Squidward: Because you'll bite the dust.

What do you get when you eat a frozen Krabby Patty?

Frostbite.

Why did SpongeBob crawl under his food?

He doesn't like to overeat.

Why did Patrick refuse to crawl under the table?

He didn't want to be underfed.

What did SpongeBob say to the Krabby Patty?

"Pleased to eat you!"

What did the Krabby Patties say when they saw their friend in Patrick's hands?

"What's eating him?"

SpongeBob: What do you call a huge lizard that only eats in the evening?

Patrick: A dinnersaur.

Squidward: Did the spatula decide to catch the patty or drop it?

SpongeBob: It left it up in the air.

SpongeBob: Why did the customer step on his check?

Squidward: He wanted to foot the bill.

Squidward: Knock-knock.
Customer: Who's there?
Squidward: Men.
Customer: Men who?
Squidward: Menu, or are you ready to order?

Mr. Krabs: What's the difference between a wiener and someone who grabs all the spots?

SpongeBob: One's a hotdog and the other's a dot hog.

Mrs. Puff: Which fruit is the saddest?

SpongeBob: The blueberry.

Sandy: What did you lose at the Chum Bucket?

SpongeBob: My appetite.

SpongeBob: How did Patrick get food all over the mirror?

Squidward: He was trying to feed his face.

Patrick: What happened when the patty met the bun?

SpongeBob: It was lunch at first sight.

SpongeBob: What do you get when you cross a gull and a swallow?

Sandy: A sea gulp.

Patrick: Which part of the ocean is the thirstiest?

SpongeBob: The Gulp of Mexico.

SpongeBob: Knock-knock.
Customer: Who's there?
SpongeBob: Goblet.
Customer: Goblet who?
SpongeBob: Gobble it down—it's a Krabby Patty!

How did the Krabby Patty feel when Squidward left him on the grill too long?

It really burned him up.

Why did Patrick sign up for percussion lessons?

Mr. Krabs told him to drum up new business.

Is it hard to guess Patrick's favorite dessert?

No, it's a piece of cake.

Why did SpongeBob eat the Mystery Patty from the top down?

He wanted to get to the bottom of it.

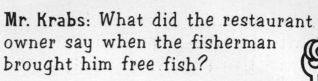

Mr. Krabs: What did the restaurant owner say when the fisherman brought him free fish?

Squidward: "What's the catch?"

What's the difference between a mini-Krabby Patty and the sound a duck with a cold makes?

One's a quick snack and the other's a sick quack.

SpongeBob: Why did the frozen boy patty throw himself at the frozen girl patty?

Sandy: He wanted to break the ice.

Mr. Krabs: Why did you paint squares on the customer?

Patrick: Uh, because he said, "Check, please."

Why did SpongeBob throw paint
during his fry cook's exam?

He wanted to pass with flying colors.

Patrick: Why can't boiling pots be spies?
SpongeBob: They always blow their covers.

Why did SpongeBob jump over the eating area?

Mr. Krabs told him to clear the table.

SpongeBob: Why did the soup refuse to leave the pot?

Sandy: It was chicken.

Mr. Krabs: Why do stand-up comics love to have eggs in their audiences?

SpongeBob: It's easy to make them crack up.

Why did Patrick bring a shovel to the Krusty Krab?

SpongeBob told him to dig in.

SpongeBob: How did the water feel after it washed the dishes?
Squidward: Drained.

What happened after Squidward said he'd never, ever eat alphabet soup?

He ate his words.

Patrick: How did the pancake's comedy act go over?
SpongeBob: It fell flat.

Patrick: How did that leave the pancake?
SpongeBob: Flat broke.

Why does Patrick fill his house with bread in the winter?

So it'll be nice and toasty.

Why did SpongeBob train a mouse to clean the Krusty Krab?

He wanted it to be squeaky clean.

Patrick: Why don't patties sleep on the grill?

SpongeBob: Because they'd spend the whole night tossing and burning.

Why did
SpongeBob
think the grill
was angry?

It flared up at him.

Pearl: Why didn't the ketchup tell the mustard how he felt about her?

SpongeBob: His feelings were all bottled up.

Mr. Krabs: How did the ice cream react to leaving the freezer?

Squidward: It had a total meltdown.

SpongeBob: How did the napkin do in the poker game?

Squidward: It folded.

SpongeBob: What do you get when you cross a bird with a chili?

Squidward: A woodpepper.

Why did SpongeBob tie
a rope to the seat and
lift it to the ceiling?
Mr. Krabs told him to
pull up a chair.

Pearl: Why was the
pepper exhausted?

Mrs. Puff: Because it
had been put through
the mill.

Why did Mr. Krabs put all his money in the freezer?

Because he wanted cold cash.

Why was the patty grouchy?

It got up on the wrong side of the bread.

Patrick: How did the milkshake feel about his time in the blender?

SpongeBob: He had mixed feelings about it.

What's Plankton's favorite kind of bread?

Shortbread.

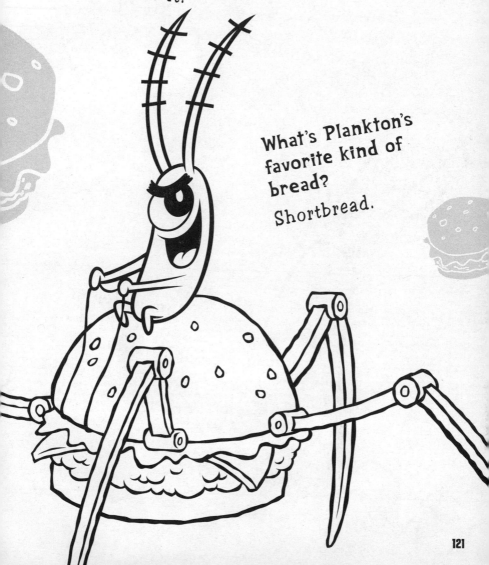

Sandy: When does butter do its best?

SpongeBob: When it's on a roll.

What did Patrick say to the customer when he filled in for Squidward?

"May I taste your order?"

Mr. Krabs: How did the onion feel about being sliced?

SpongeBob: It really got under his skin.

SpongeBob: When does food make you itch?

Patrick: When you make it from scratch.

How does SpongeBob say good-bye to the patties when he leaves work?

"Spatulater!"

Why did SpongeBob toss a sandwich at Sandy on her birthday?

He wanted to throw her a surprise patty.

Why did SpongeBob put a circle of Krusty Krab sandwiches around his house?

He wanted to have an outdoor patty-o.

What do they call a stall in the Krusty Krab restroom?

A Krabby Potty.

SpongeBob: Knock-knock.
Customer: Who's there?
SpongeBob: Stan.
Customer: Stan who?
SpongeBob: Stan in line to order, please.

SpongeBob: Knock-knock.
Squidward: Who's there?
SpongeBob: Betty.
Squidward: Betty who?
SpongeBob: Bet he orders
another Krabby Patty.

Patrick: Knock-knock.
Squidward: Who's there?
Patrick: Al.
Squidward: Al who?
Patrick: Al have a double
  Krabby Patty with cheese.

Mr. Krabs: Knock-knock.
SpongeBob: Who's there?
Mr. Krabs: Donna.
SpongeBob: Donna who?
Mr. Krabs: Don a uniform before you start work.

Patrick: Which big, mean fish bakes the best bread?

SpongeBob: The Great Wheat Shark.

Why did SpongeBob jump up on the stove? He wanted to play King of the Grill.

How would SpongeBob like working in a ship's kitchen?

It'd be right up his galley.

SpongeBob: What do you call a tortilla filled with ice?

Sandy: A brrr-ito.

SpongeBob: What do chickens eat when they wake up?
Sandy: Peckfast.

Why did Patrick attach four tires and a steering wheel to the table?

Because Mr. Krabs told him to bus it.

Mr. Krabs: What kind of cup is impossible to drink from?
Squidward: A hiccup.

Sandy: Why did the piece of corn try to join the army?
Squidward: Because he was already a kernel.

Patrick: What do ghosts order with their Krabby Patties?

SpongeBob: French frights.

Why did SpongeBob put a barbecue grill on the roof of his house?

He wanted to raise the steaks.

Sandy: Where do vegetables go to kiss?

SpongeBob: The mushroom.

Why did Patrick throw the T-bone in a blender?

He wanted to make a chocolate milksteak.

Why did Patrick try to have a conversation with a can of beans?

Because he'd heard there was a story called *Jack and the Beans Talk*.

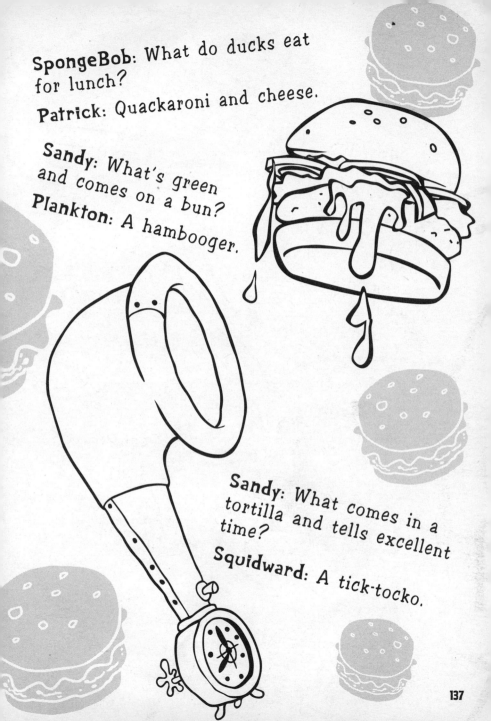

SpongeBob: What do ducks eat for lunch?

Patrick: Quackaroni and cheese.

Sandy: What's green and comes on a bun?

Plankton: A hambooger.

Sandy: What comes in a tortilla and tells excellent time?

Squidward: A tick-tocko.

SpongeBob: If corn could talk, what kind of voice would it have?

Mr. Krabs: Husky.

SpongeBob: What would it say?

Mr. Krabs: "Shucks, I'm all ears."

SpongeBob: What did the waiter say to the frog?

Squidward: "You want flies with that?"

What did SpongeBob say when he ran out of cabbage?

"That's the last slaw."

I'm full!

THE END

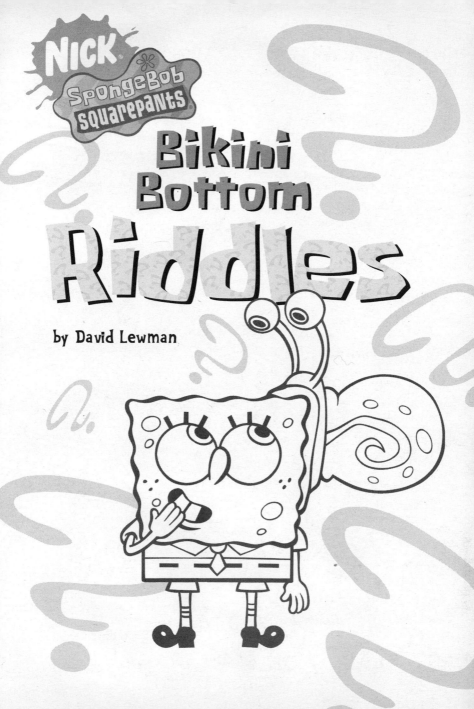

NICK
SpongeBob SquarePants

Bikini Bottom
Riddles

by David Lewman

Why doesn't SpongeBob have to pay his electric bill?

Because his pineapple house never runs out of juice!

Sandy: Knock-knock.

Patrick : Who's there?

Sandy: Funnel.

Patrick Funnel who?

Sandy: Fun'll break out the minute SpongeBob gets here!

Why is Sandy Friends with SpongeBob and Patrick?
Because squirrels love nuts!

Why does SpongeBob love mushrooms?
Because there's FUN in every FUNgus!

Why does SpongeBob keep toys in the refrigerator?
So he can play it cool.

Why did Plankton push a toy toward Patrick with a stick?
He was trying to poke fun at him.

146

Patrick: Knock-knock.

Sandy: Who's there?

Patrick : Plane.

Sandy: Plane who?

Patrick : Playin' with SpongeBob is my favorite thing to do!

Why did SpongeBob set up his games outside a haunted house?
He wanted to play by the ghouls.

Patrick: Knock-knock.
SpongeBob: Who's there?
Patrick: Ice.
SpongeBob: Ice who?
Patrick: Ice cream, please!

Why do SpongeBob
and Patrick like to eat
together?
So they can be taste buds.

Patrick: Knock-knock.

SpongeBob: Who's there?

Patrick: Pile.

SpongeBob: Pile who?

Patrick: Pie'll go great with this ice cream!

Why does Patrick always fall asleep when SpongeBob beats him in a game?
He's a snore loser.

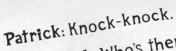

Patrick: Knock-knock.

SpongeBob: Who's there?

Patrick: Sir.

SpongeBob: Sir who?

Patrick: Surprise! It's me!

Why did Patrick build a house out of cheese?
So he'd have cottage cheese.

IF Patrick were an outlaw, who would he be?
Belly the Kid.

What is Patrick's breakfast specialty?
Belchin' waffles.

Who invented the gas-powered telephone?
Alexander Graham Belch.

What did Patrick win at the belching contest?
A burp certificate.

Why did Patrick climb up the side of the Fish?
He wanted to be king of the gill.

Why are mornings tough in Patrick's house?
You always get off to a rocky start.

What kind of stone is the best to sleep on?
Bedrock.

Why did Patrick move out from under the green stone?
It turned out to be a sham rock.

What do you get when you
cross Squidward with a wasp?
A grumble bee.

IF Squidward
were a plant,
what kind
would he be?
A grumble weed.

What group did Squidward join
when he was young?
The Snub Scouts.

Squidward: Knock-knock.

Mr. Krabs: Who's there?

Squidward: Snob.

Mr. Krabs: Snob who?

Squidward: This knob's so greasy I can't open the door.

What crime did the police arrest Squidward for?

Six armed snobberies.

Why did SpongeBob strap a watch to his shoe?
So he was always on time.

Squidward: Knock-knock.

SpongeBob: Who's there?

Squidward: Walleye.

SpongeBob: Walleye who?

Squidward: While I nap, you work.

What does Squidward use to turn his boat?
The sneering wheel.

Why did SpongeBob have to stop driving at the end of the day?
He ran out of class.

How does Mrs. Puff feel when she gives exams?
Testy.

Why did Mrs. Puff feel crazy after SpongeBob's license test?
He drove her up a wall.

Why can't Mrs. Puff understand SpongeBob?
Because she never knows what he's driving at.

What do you call someone with a boating license in Bikini Bottom?
A deep-sea driver.

What does Mr. Krabs love to drive?
A hard bargain.

How is Plankton like Squidward's ink?
They're both little squirts.

Why won't Plankton ever make a big splash?
Because he's a little drip.

What does Plankton chew between meals?
Bubble chum.

Why did the Fish stop eating worms?
He was trying to lose bait.

Why are Fish always
making excuses?
To get off the hook.

What do you call
baby Fish in sauce?
Tartar tots.

Which fish is the cheapest?
The stingy ray.

Which kind of seal is the most musical?
The harp seal.

What did the seal princess lose at the ball?
Her glass Flipper.

What do fish ride at the playground?
The teeter-tartar.

Which fish is the heaviest?
The goldfish.

Which fish is the most fetching?
The dogfish.

What did the witch do to the Fish?
She cast a smell on him.

What did SpongeBob get when he tried using karate on a pig?
A pork chop.

How did the hammerhead shark do on his exam?
He nailed it.

Which vegetable is the funniest?
The artijoke.

Why did the tomato fall on Patrick?
It wanted to squish upon a star.

What did SpongeBob say when he found the kitchen floor covered in tomatoes? "There's something squishy going on here."

What's brown and delicious and really dangerous?
A chocolate milk shark.

Which kind of salt should never be used during meals?
The somersault.

How did the salt feel when it met the French Fries?
Shaken.

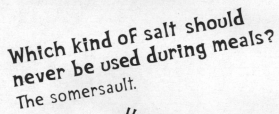

Why was
SpongeBob
afraid of the
Krabby Patty
buns?
They looked seedy.

How do you get answers
out of a Krabby Patty?
You grill it.

What is SpongeBob's favorite bedtime story?
Hansel and Griddle.

Why did SpongeBob add bubble soap to his pancakes?
He wanted to blow his stack.

How did the Krabby Patty Feel by the end of the workday?
Totally Fried.

How did Squidward Feel about the world's tiniest pickle?
It was no big dill.

Which sea can give you gas?
The CaribBEAN.

Which ocean can make you laugh?
The Atlantickle.

Which ocean is the most detailed?
The Specific Ocean.

Why did the whale drink hot water?
She wanted to blow off steam.

Which fish is best at answering doors?
The halibutler.

Which fish is the best at boxing?
The sockeye salmon.

Which fish has the shortest temper?
The snapper.

Which Fish does the best imitations?
The parrot Fish.

Which Fish is the clumsiest?
The Flounder.

Which Fish makes the best shoes?
The sole.

What's it called when you trip in Bikini Bottom?

A waterfall.

What's the best kind of
water to sleep on?
Spring water.

What's the best kind of
water to dance on?
Tap water.

Sandy: Did you hear about the robber with the messy hair?
SpongeBob: Yeah, he was thrown in gel.

Patrick: What did the key say to the door?
Mr. Krabs: "Things are locking up."

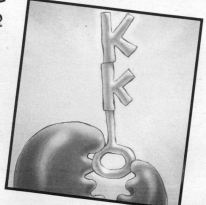

SpongeBob: Knock-knock.

Sandy: Who's there?

SpongeBob: Beach.

Sandy: Beach who?

SpongeBob: Beach you to the Goo Lagoon!

Why doesn't Bubble Buddy like to bake?
He's afraid of rolling pins.

Which musical notes does Bubble Buddy like least?
The sharps.

What kind of candy should you never give to Bubble Buddy?

A lolli*pop*.

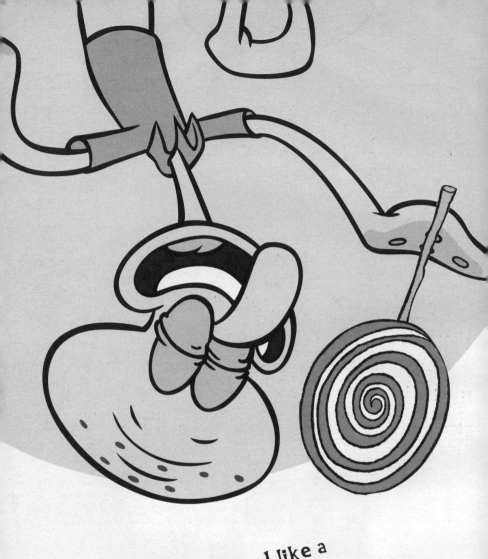

Why is Squidward like a lollipop on the ceiling?

He's stuck-up.

What do sea snakes do
after a fight?
They hiss and make up.

Which snake makes
the best dessert?
The pie-thon.

Why did Patchy the Pirate
jiggle the treasure chest?
He wanted to shake his booty.

What says "ahr,"
steals treasure, and
tastes delicious?
A cherry pirate.

What is Patchy the Pirate's best basketball move?
His hook shot.

Why did SpongeBob go to JellyFish Fields?
To hear the latest buzz.

SpongeBob: Knock-knock.

Patrick: Who's there?

SpongeBob: Sam.

Patrick: Sam who?

SpongeBob: Salmon are coming this way—let's leave.

THE END